Ferociously
Close to Home

Cheers,
Dell and
Audrey!

John McPherson

**Other *Close to Home* Books
by John McPherson**

Close to Home
One Step Closer to Home
Dangerously Close to Home
Home: The Final Frontier
The Honeymoon Is Over
The Silence of the Lamberts
Striking Close to Home
The Close to Home Survival Guide
Close to Home Uncut
The Scourge of the Vinyl Car Seats
Close to Home Exposed

Treasury Collections
Close to Home Revisited
Close to Home Unplugged

Also from John McPherson
High School Isn't Pretty
Close to Home: A Book of Postcards
The Barber of Bingo
The Get Well Book
Give Mommy the Superglue and Other Tips on Surviving Parenthood

Ferociously Close to Home

A Close to Home Collection by John McPherson

**Andrews McMeel
Publishing**

Kansas City

03 04 05 06 07 BBG 10 9 8 7 6 5 4 3 2 1

ISBN: 0-7407-3812-7

Library of Congress Catalog Control Number: 2003106555

Close to Home may be viewed on the Internet at
www.uComics.com.

Visit the **Close to Home** Web store at
www.closetohome.com.

E-mail John McPherson at
closetohome@compuserve.com.

─── **ATTENTION: SCHOOLS AND BUSINESSES** ───

Andrews McMeel books are available at quantity discounts with bulk purchase for educational, business, or sales promotional use. For information, write to: Special Sales Department, Andrews McMeel Publishing, 4520 Main Street, Kansas City, Missouri 64111.

For Nancy Butcher

"The middle is regular carpeting. The perimeter rung is Velcro,
and the twins are wearing Velcro boots. Needless to say,
life has gotten a whole lot easier around here!"

Quickly deciding that her date is a loser, Brenda makes a tactical maneuver to keep the evening as short as possible.

"I'll give you each a three-second head start then I'll send Choonga up after you. If he catches you before you reach the top, you owe me twenty laps around the track."

". . . So, while you were sleeping, I talked to the doctors and they worked it out so you can still keep building the deck when you get home."

9

To her horror, Bernice triggers the store's Used-the-Rest-Room-but-Didn't-Make-a-Purchase alarm.

**"Whoa! He, Gina . . . I, uh . . . really messed up!
I swear to you, I will never, ever, ever forget
your birthday again, honey!"**

With the season winding down, Lenny became
more determined than ever to catch a
Mark McGwire home run ball.

"People can talk all they want about fancy electronic security systems, Mr. Greenstead, but nothing beats this tried-and-true method."

"... so now when we need clean sheets, we just turn the crank! This roll should last us three years!"

"We initially got her to tackle the problem of raccoons raiding our garbage, but Queenie is so affectionate with the kids that we decided to keep the lovable old scamp!"

At the National Institute for Retraining Husbands to Hear Their Wives' Voices.

For those desperate moments when the aisle is blocked by meal carts, Northmont Air devised emergency rest room tunnels.

"Lois, I am fine! We planned this golf vacation two years ago! If you think I'm going to let a little back trouble ruin it, you're crazy!"

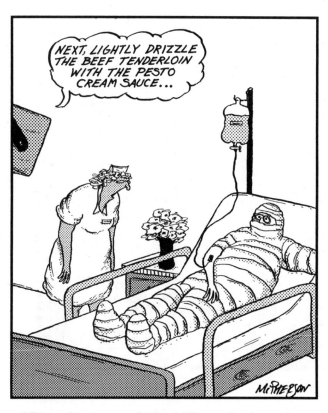

"Our cable is out of whack. The only channel we get is the Gourmet Food Channel."

Acting on a whim, Ray discovers that his TV remote works on the stadium superscreen.

To prevent them from being taken advantage of by unruly students, substitute teachers at Glencrest Junior High underwent an extensive makeup session each morning.

"We've devised a fair way to determine which six employees will have to work over Columbus Day weekend. You're up against Gloria Hudak at 12:30."

"Will you shut up about how far it is to the snack bar?! It cost me $300 for these seats!"

"It's got a built-in homing device. Once every twenty-four hours it seeks out the largest cellulite deposit in the house."

"I did a time and cost analysis on the garage.
It makes more sense to add on to it
than to clean it out."

"Ramona, I was *totally* out of line when I called your mother an obnoxious, psychotic water buffalo. She's a sweet, caring individual. Now put down the leaf blower, Honey."

"Okay, Mr. Hudak, let's try it with the training device in place this time. Remember, keep your head down."

Thanks to the same technology that bank drive-through windows rely on, frenzied parents no longer need worry about their kids missing the school bus.

A seldom-considered further consequence of the year 2000 computer glitch.

"It's a genetically engineered maple tree. It provides more shade than a regular maple, but has only six really huge, easy-to-dispose-of leaves."

"We need to try something a bit more aggressive,
Mr. Credman. Let us know the instant
you feel your headache start to ease."

"Well, too bad, Honey. The only diaper changing
station they have is in the women's room.
Looks like it's up to you."

"Happy birthday, Ed! Well, come on! Try it out!
You'll think you're jogging through a beautiful pine forest!"

Philharmonic promotions

Mr. Sinclair's woodshop class was slowly starting to catch on to his weekly "field trip" scam.

To help them stave off empty-nest syndrome in later years, the Martinos made a point of recording every unpleasant parenting experience.

"Calm down, Louise. I'm sure it's just part of the after-dinner entertainment."

"This is just as effective, without the hassle of a toddler gate. Anytime he gets near the stairs, the lion head roars and scares him back."

"Now watch carefully as Dr. Keeler staples the insurance claim form to the patient's admission form."

"It drops about a half-inch per minute. It was the only thing I could come up with to control Jerry's addiction to surfing the Net."

"Okay, you caught us. But admit it! You've been feeling a whole lot better since we hooked you up to the 'machine' two weeks ago."

In an effort to reduce injuries, many high school football conferences have adopted the two-handed tickle-tackling rule.

"Mine's the 'Howard Stern' in the back row."

Arnie has the misfortune of hitting into one of the course's challenging new sickle traps.

After the 117th Monica Lewinsky costume, Frieda and Glenn Daggett lash out.

"Mr. Weingard, our contract with you guarantees to cure your baldness. At no point does it promise to regrow hair."

The Fulkersons finally devised a way to keep their teenagers from monopolizing the bathroom.

To keep pace with the endless requests for donations to employees' birthday and get-well gifts, management devised the hourly Gift Trolley.

"I tell ya, Helen, I rue the day that I signed us up for those Riverdance lessons."

"Barbara, I warned you not to go in there while you were still dizzy from the Scrambler."

The rivalry between Dr. Miller and Dr. Clindale reaches a crescendo.

Midway into the third period, members of the Vancouver Canucks and Philadelphia Flyers make a startling archaeological discovery.

Ferndale High wisely equipped all of its driver's ed cars with ejection seats.

Though it was only his second day on the job, employees were already getting bad vibes about the new division chief.

"Did I mention the comment I made at last night's school board meeting?"

"He's got Raffi-itis, Mrs. Fernweld. There are seven kids' songs stuck in his head that we'll try to blast out using some Jimi Hendrix tunes."

**At the 2003 Parenting Olympics:
Port-a-Crib Assembly Race**

Thanks to Toddler-Cam, the Fergusons were able to track down virtually any object their eighteen-month-old got his hands on.

"Darn it all, Melissa! Take it easy on the toilet paper! Ya think they just *give* that stuff away?!"

"Before we get you down, we need to take a few photos for insurance purposes, ma'am."

"I read about this in the company newsletter. They're trying to get us all into shape for the Corporate Challenge next spring."

Mike pulls the old "fake splinter" gag in woodshop.

Bernie and Clarice Waller: the unfortunate down-stairs neighbors of a member of *Stomp*

The editor of *Consumer Reports* experiences a momentary lapse of reason.

Karl devises a way to enhance his on-line chatting experience.

"...and when you come back and show me that
your parents have signed your report cards,
then the cuffs can come off."

Although her performance review hadn't begun yet,
Nancy sensed the worst.

Thanks to his new pop-out fullness indicator,
Andy was able to leave the Thanksgiving table
satisfied, not stuffed.

"When we go on a trip, we just shovel the kitty litter off to the side and . . . voilà! . . . a place to stash our valuables where no burglar would ever look!"

A failed experiment in high school sports: cross-country cheerleaders

"Oh, Jack, calm down. It won't scratch the car, and it'll sure make the fourteen-hour drive to your parents' a lot more tolerable for all of us."

No one could stretch Thanksgiving leftovers like
Glenda Richardson.

54

Bruce tries out his new combination mouse/massager.

When high school students dream

"Essentially, it's voodoo for a good purpose.
We'll soak this replica of you in our mini-whirlpool
for twenty-four hours, and in six weeks your back
will be as good as new."

"Well, if you're the *real* Santa Claus then I guess
you won't mind if I take your fingerprints and
compare them to the ones I lifted off my
Barbie's Dream House last Christmas."

"Well?! Don't just stand there! Get over there and tell them they're in our seats!"

"The amazing thing is that he's doing it all without having had his afternoon nap!"

Having placed the Inflate-a-Car® in the mall parking lot at 3 A.M., Carol had shrewdly reserved herself a primo parking spot.

"For heaven's sake! You mean all you did was type in Amazon.com?!!"

"We came up with a way for you to work off your medical expenses."

Nine years of living in a subdivision with 729 children in it had finally pushed Pam and Joe Remley over the edge.

"And you say you first noticed it about six weeks ago when he started watching *Teletubbies*?"

How teachers decide which students to call on in class

A leading group of gangsta rappers attempts to break into the lucrative Christmas music market.

"Now calm down, Mr. Gormsteen. I'll be right here the entire time, and remember, you'll get 25 percent off your next bill."

To help simplify the holidays, many families are opting for built-in, pre-decorated Christmas trees.

"... real rock ... real ... *fake rock with a hide-a-key!* ... real rock ...
uhh ... real rock! ... *fake!* .. real ..."

In a cruel abuse of the Christmas spirit, students in Mr. Egmont's geometry class discover that his gifts to them contain a surprise midterm.

"Roger, never mind! I found the airline tickets under my blouse on the bed!"

"I'm sorry, folks, but due to the extremely crowded conditions in the mall, we're requiring that all shoppers wear corsets."

The annual Christmas bonus check wind chamber is always a big hit at Kelpman Industries.

"Oh, George, don't be such a Scrooge! Fifty dollars is very reasonable for a chocolate bar that size, and it's for a good cause."

"After you open your first gift, you write a thank-you note for it and scan the note into the Gift-O-Matic©, at which time another gift will be dispensed."

"He read an article in *Home Handyman Digest* that says we can save 20 percent on our heating bill this way."

Tony rebels against the ludicrously high price of theater popcorn.

"Whoa! Not so fast! *First* you fill out your insurance forms, *then* you get your medicine!"

A team of prominent psychologists studies the phenomenon of compulsive e-mail forwarding.

Seeing the salesman approaching, Brenda activates
her artificial screaming toddler.

By soaking the telephone in pure bear musk,
Carl was able to reduce the family's phone bill
by 83 percent.

73

Many opera companies now provide interpreters for the culturally impaired.

Lanny triggers the health club's offensive odor alarm.

Overcome by curiosity, Milt discovers what happens when
you search the word "Yahoo" at Yahoo.com.

Tired of having the kids constantly streaming through the kitchen, the Searsons wisely installed a bypass tunnel.

With ski conditions often being unpredictable, many skiers are relying on personal snowblowing systems.

The two members of the bowling team knew this was a once-in-a-lifetime opportunity.

"Don't worry. The plants, the legs—they're all fake. We just put them in to keep people from walking their dogs in our yard."

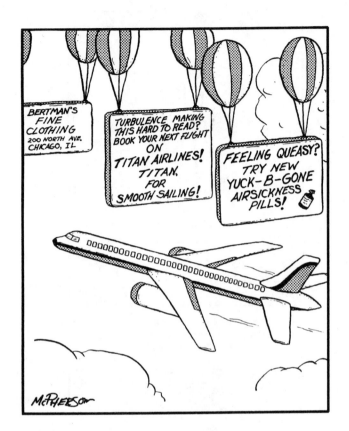

"Occasionally we have some plumbing problems with the bathroom up above in 2-C. Look, do you want the apartment or not?"

"All I can say is, it's been a very long football season."

Although they hadn't said it out loud, Carol and Steve couldn't help but think about the endorsement potential that Kyle's birthmark presented.

How most high school students choose a college

Alex Trebek's recurring nightmare

"You'll be able to donate a pint of blood in a
fraction of the time it would have taken
the old way."

Knowing that she had already blown her driver's
test with her lousy parallel parking, Karen decided
to have a little fun with the examiner.

"To help you communicate during your root canal, we've created this chart of commonly used patient phrases."

Responding to fans' complaints that the puck is too hard to follow, the NHL unveils its new **Puck Enhancement System**.

"...And it is now with heavy hearts that we bid a final farewell to our friend, Eddie the Human Cannonball."

"Your prescription will be $80, or if you want, you can try our grab bag for $5 and hope you get lucky."

"Thank you, Barbara. Next, David Lombardo will give his presentation on the ancient city of Pompeii."

As a service to their weight-conscious customers, all Food Queen grocery stores have installed Thigh-Cams at key locations.

"I warned you not to order the prime rib
this late in the evening."

English teacher Ramona Gelch felt that a visual aid was essential to enhancing her students' appreciation of *Moby-Dick*.

"The dam has burst, and we've used every last sandbag in the county! For the love of God, Marilyn, let us have your Beanie Babies!!"

"Oh gosh, ma'am, I'm sorry! I forgot to take the little magnetic security thingy off your CD!"

Linda's nine-year racket for getting out of speeding tickets comes crashing to an end.

"Of *course* we care about the headaches and eye-strain you data processors are experiencing. That's precisely why we've installed ibuprofen dispensers on every monitor."

Knowing that he might be away on business when Colleen went into labor, Glen had prepared a labor-coaching video ahead of time.

With football season over with, the Dagners and the Kellmans looked for any excuse to have a tailgate party.

"Come on, Dad! We want to see if you can beat the mailman's time of thirty-seven minutes and sixteen seconds."

Stu and Reggie orchestrate an elaborate
cheating scam.

A grim sense of foreboding struck Glenda and Ted
as they opening the fourth copy of *Can This
Marriage Be Saved?*

"Denise, could you please go over to the storage cabinet and get the *large* tub of Vaseline?"

Kodakaphobia: the inability to throw out any of the hundreds of cute kid photos you receive in friends' Christmas cards

The ushers' new collection plate backboards increased donations to the church by 127 percent.

Angered by Mr. Torkelson's new mandatory overtime policy, everyone in the office chipped in to send him a Wedgie-Gram.

Life with an eBay addict

"And here all this time I just thought we had a lousy sketch artist."

"They take a few days to get used to, but eventually you'll appreciate how much quieter apartment living is with rubber floors."

"I'm playing darts against a bus driver
in Malaysia!"

"Geesh! Your other ski *still* hasn't hit the bottom!"

"Relax. That's only temporary until your follow-up surgery in June."

"According to the infomercial, it takes only a few nights to train yourself to use it, and you can lose six pounds a week."

The ugly side of telecommuting

Before performing a vasectomy, Dr. Credman always played the same song to help get himself psyched up.

Striving to maintain its fan base in the wake of the lockout and Michael Jordan's retirement, the NBA makes some drastic changes to its format.

"When he first said he wanted to try home-brewing, I thought, 'Finally! A retirement hobby to keep him occupied and give me some peace and quiet!'"

"Health and fitness books? Sure. Follow this line of hurdles, climb the rope to the second floor, crawl through the big pipe, scale the climbing wall ..."

"Why pay $289 to have cruise control installed? You wanna go 65? Grab the rock marked 65 and set it on the gas pedal! You wanna go 55, you grab ..."

Realty ad copywriting 201

Knowledgeable students are able to trace the history of the school's most memorable food fights by studying the cafeteria ceiling.

Twenty-seven percent of all Americans suffer from Compulsive Checkout Lingering Syndrome.

"She needs to be immobile for six weeks, after which we can upgrade her to a swimming cast."

Uncomfortable with any kind of confrontation,
Walt relied on Mr. Chuckles to lay off employees.

Joanne's new perfume was an instant hit with Al.

Teacher conference days: the *real* story

The grocery superstores continue to expand their product lines.

In an unprecedented display of respect for a professional athlete, Michael Jordan's number 23 is retired from all aspects of American culture.

"It's working! Productivity in this department is up 87 percent!"

The downside of home schooling

Worried that Jeremy might fall asleep in the car and blow his nap at home, Becky activates her Toddler Anti-Snooze System.

With unemployment dipping below one percent in many parts of the U.S., some employers are taking drastic steps to fill positions.

"Headquarters, this is unit 29 at 398 Maple! We've got a man down! Repeat, *Man down!* Requesting immediate backup!"

Helen's hectic life became noticeably simpler once she equipped her toddlers' coats with Zipper-matic™.

"Since today's service is being videotaped for commemorative purposes, we ask that the following parishioners refrain from singing during the hymns: Shirley Garkman, Butch Swarsky, Linda Mutlin ..."

"Jeepers! Is it 12:25 already? A half-hour just isn't enough time for lunch, is it?"

"Right now the baby is *not* in the proper position
for delivery, but I'm confident it will shift
in time for your due date."

"Will you quit buying these darned 'LOVE'
stamps? I feel like a hypocrite whenever I
pay the electric bill!"

Let's face it. Everybody does this when they're assigned a 2,000-word term paper.

Mike would know better than to raise his hand the next time Mr. Femcod asked for a volunteer to erase the blackboard.

E-mail anxiety

Working relentlessly through the night at the superintendent's house, a team of students hopes to dupe him into declaring a snow day.

Specialized Day Care Centers

To help discourage office romances, employees at Witten Industries were required to wear designated costumes each day.

Concerned about recent criticism of Tinky Winky, the producers of *Teletubbies* attempt to toughen his image.

Equipped with a series of tiny microphones under her fingernails and a 200-watt amplifier, Mrs. Raffner relished the moment she spotted a student dozing off.

As soon as the **Realtor** showed them the house's hinged facade, allowing furniture to be easily moved inside, the **Scrodners** knew they had found their dream home.

In an effort to compete with Apple's new line of colorful iMacs, a leading PC manufacturer introduces its line of scratch 'n' sniff tropical fruit-scented monitors.

With the meeting dragging on interminably, Darrel hit the secret burst-water-pipe button.

"Well, we had a little excitement at this afternoon's bridge club."

Rather than simply reading an employee's performance review to him, Mr. Quidler liked delivering it via a rousing game of charades.

"G'day, mate! First time to Australia?"

127

Prior to visiting Orlando, the La Clairs had wisely purchased a copy of *The Blueprints of Disney's Utility Tunnels.*

129

"Whatever surprise you uncovered in there, it certainly can't top this!
I found part of an old dollar bill dated 1903 underneath the wallpaper
in the dining room!"

"Jerry! The sunscreen! Drop the sunscreen!"

"The doctor says you'll get used to them in no time, but you need to be *careful*."

The Fegley High Drama Club presents its adaptation of *Jaws*.

Always striving to improve customer satisfaction, Titan Airlines equips all of its jetliners with bay windows.

And then one day, while watching reruns of *Hollywood Squares*, manager Dick Sheldon was struck with the solution to the company's space-utilization problem.

Equipped with a canister of compressed air and some rubber tubing, Wayne was able to shave six strokes off his game.

As she scattered Leon's ashes off the
Oakmont Bridge, Tina realized she had
completely forgotten about his glass eye.

Thanks to her new Commuter-Chute 2000,
Brenda was able to sleep twelve minutes later
each morning.

Andy liked to wait until his victim was 95 percent done before he hit the button.

"You hop in there, she'll untie you, and then you tell her you were kidnapped over the weekend and couldn't get the term paper done."

"Before you say a word, answer me this:
How would you like to never have to deal with
door-to-door salesmen again?"

"Now, we need to test your eyesight at night, in a driving rainstorm, while a deer crosses the road, and your wife is ticked because you missed the last rest stop."

"Calm down guys! They're not poisonous, and I think they'll inspire you to set new records in long-jumping."

For those mornings when all she could manage to throw on was a ratty T-shirt and sweats, Nancy relied on her **Classy-Bus-Stop-Mom Facade™**.

Rotert Industries institutes its new mandatory overtime policy.

"I don't think it's quite ready, Mr. Heffner. Why don't you have a seat in our waiting area and enjoy some coffee on us?"

"He's two and a half days old and he's already had nine time-outs!"

Eighteen years of working in the corporate world had left Eric severely cubicle dependent.

"And now, with the help of his friend Steve,
Mort will hole-out for his final round."

"We've got a few more passengers than usual, and we want to make sure we're able to clear the Rockies."

"I'll just be a second. My insoles get really sweaty by lunchtime, so I just want to zap them a bit to dry them out."

"I'm tellin' ya, Shirley, it's drivin' me nuts! Fifteen times I bait the trap with a piece of fudge, and fifteen times the fudge is gone, the trap is sprung, and **NO MOUSE!**"

Woodshop student Danny Curdleman demonstrates his combination bird feeder/napkin holder.

Mega Mart is plunged into chaos when, acting on a secret intuitive signal, every toddler in the store simultaneously throws a tantrum.

Bernie lashes out at management's new no-food-at-your-desk policy.

Not wanting to look like a spaz at the prom, Roger equipped himself with a Dance-Matic 2000™.

At the Spandex™ Testing Facility